Jesus said,

# I NEVER KNEW YOU

PALMETTO
PUBLISHING

Charleston, SC
www.PalmettoPublishing.com

*Jesus Said, I Never Knew You*
Copyright © 2022 by Larry K. Vliem

First Edition

Paperback: 979-8-88590-798-9
eBook: 979-8-88590-799-6

# Jesus said,
# I NEVER
# KNEW YOU

By Larry K. Vliem

# PREFACE

"Not everyone who says to me, 'Lord, Lord,' will enter the kingdom of heaven, but the one who does the will of my Father who is in heaven" (Matthew 7:21). Listen carefully to these words, "On that day many will say to me, 'Lord, Lord, did we not prophesy in your name, and do many mighty works in your name?' And then I will declare to them, 'I never knew you; depart from me, you workers of lawlessness" (Matthew 7:22-23).

Matthew 7:15 gives us clues as to whom these people who will not enter the kingdom of heaven are, "beware of false prophets, who come to you in sheep's clothing but inwardly are ravenous wolves."

God sees the inward reflection of a person's heart. Only He can judge one's heart, and only that person can know if their heart is right with God. The Bible is the mirror to your heart and when you study the Bible each day you will begin to see clearly what your heart should look like and your heart will then become pleasing to God.

1 John 5:13 says "I write these things to you who believe in the name of the Son of God, that you may know

that you have eternal life." This is the focus of this book, that you may know you have eternal life.

# INTRODUCTION

According to John 3:1–3, "Now there was a man of the Pharisees named Nicodemus, a ruler of the Jews. The man came to Jesus by night and said to him, 'Rabbi, we know you are a teacher come from God, for no one can do these sights that you do unless God is with him.' Jesus answered him, 'Truly, truly I say to you, unless one is born again, he cannot see the kingdom of God.'"

There is concern that there is a misunderstanding of what it means to be born again, as it was to Nicodemus, so in John 3:5–8, Jesus explained to him what it meant.

Even after the resurrection of Jesus, the human family remained confused until men like Martin Luther and Charles Wesley brought new revelation, which enlightened us to a faith-based theology; salvation is through Jesus Christ and in him alone. This gave great comfort because the human family struggled to reconcile themselves to please God. They realized it was by faith in Jesus Christ that we are saved, not by works. People took the simplicity of this new revelation and, as the leaders of old, added their ideas instead of using this new revelation to fulfill the great commission to reach others for Jesus Christ. Matthew 22: 37-40, "And he said to them, 'You shall love the Lord your God with all your heart and with all your soul and with all your mind.

This is the great and the first commandment. And the second is like it; You shall love your neighbor as yourself. On these two commandments depend all the Laws and the Prophets.'"

So when God sent His Son to live, suffer, and die on a cross for us and then raised Him from the grave, was it so we can spend our time debating religion, or is there a greater purpose? Indeed, there is; it is eternity. We get only one opportunity here on earth to get this right; there are no do overs. When you reach your eternal destination, you will not be surprised. According to Matthew 5:6, "Blessed are those who hunger and thirst after righteousness for they *shall* be filled."

These were words from my dad, as he always warned me: eternity is a long time, and there is no coming back. Back from where? Hell. When you die and are not born again you will spend eternity in hell. As a child there were many messages preached on hell. Today it is all about heaven and love, which is awesome because there is nothing like experiencing the love of Jesus, but there is more to the story. Could a loving God condemn a person to an eternal hell, or is there a hell at all? To eliminate confusion, let's see what scripture says:

Job 10:20–22: "Are not my days few? Then cease, and leave me alone, that I may find a little cheer before I go—and

I shall not return—to a land of darkness and deep shadow, the land of gloom like thick darkness, like deep shadow without orders where light is a thick darkness."

Matthew 14:41–42: "The Son of Man will send out his angels, and they will gather out of his kingdom all causes of sin and all lawbreakers, and throw them into a fiery furnace, in a place there will be weeping and gnashing of teeth."

2 Thessalonians 1:9: "They shall suffer the punishment of eternal destruction, away from the presence of the Lord and the glory of his might."

God is love, but God is also just. Hell is a consequence of rejecting Him and His word.

As I grew older and experienced the death of many loved ones, I have hoped that they have gone to heaven. Many say with certainty, "I know my loved one has gone to heaven," but do we know? What everyone believes about another when one dies gives us comfort, but only God knows what is in the heart of a person. I pose that question because where you get your instruction and understanding is critical.

As a young person, I gave my heart to Jesus, and as I continue my journey in life, there have been moments of doubt. So when scripture teaches us that we may know we have eternal life, I had to find out how. Being brought up in a family of faith, the Bible was the word of God, so that was where I got my information.

We need to have a firm foundation. Who is God? What are angels and the human family? The Bible, the Holy Scripture, was written so that a third-grader can understand it. That is important, as you will see later, but for an introduction to help give us guidance, the Holy Scriptures were written so we will be able to understand God's expectation of us. A special note of caution is absolutely critical here. The Bibles we read today are translations. Every Bible must introduce those who have translated the scriptures. The background and beliefs of these translators is absolutely critical. We can compare the different translations to discern if the content has the same meaning, just more up to date grammar as is used today. I personally conclude that the King James Version is the gold standard in making comparisons to newer translations.

As I began my study, I started to see that the scriptures were written as a whole, not as a part. Let me explain. For those who translated the scriptures, in an attempt to give guidance and understanding, they made a distinction between the Old Testament and the New Testament. I found this to be misleading. I realized that the entire scripture tells a story from the beginning to the end. I concluded there is only one Testament written by God. The entirety of scripture is critical, so He can help us know we have eternal life in heaven.

Focusing on the word *sin*, does *sin* help the reader fully understand what destroys one's relationship with God, or would it give us a clearer understanding if the translators used the terms *free will, obedience, and disobedience* instead of the word *sin*? As we understand *free will, obedience,* and *disobedience*, we will see how these three words permeate through every book of the Holy Scriptures and with God's relationship to the angels and, most importantly, where we will spend eternity. Among these three words, the most important is *free will*. So now when we define the Holy Scriptures as the Testament of God, instead of our focus on stories of the Bible, we will look for their significance, which will give us a better understanding of God's expectations for the human family.

God did not create robots; He gave the angels and the human family free will. Free will is the only way one can express love, and God loves the praises of His creations. As you continue to read on, you will see how free will, obedience, and disobedience relate to you so you may know you have eternal life.

# GOD THE FATHER

Father God is everything. Disobedience separates us from His presence and throughout eternity. He loves His creations, and He hopes that none would perish but have eternal life with Him. He gave us free will and, throughout history, tried to make a way for His creations to reconcile with Him. There were animal blood sacrifices along with severe punishments in an attempt to get the human family to obey. Finally, He sent His Son, Jesus, to make the ultimate sacrifice. Jesus's life of obedience brought severe punishment and death on a cross. Then Jesus overcame death and is now sitting on God's right hand to be our salvation. Jesus paying for our sins is the only way we can come into the presence of the Most Holy Father; there is *no* other way.

This predicate is why Jesus says, "If you love me, you will obey and keep my commandments." Write these commandments on your heart and hunger and thirst for righteousness. You are getting ready to spend eternity in the presence of the Most Holy God and going to experience unexplainable love.

We believe in the Trinity—God the Father, God the Son, and God the Holy Spirit—yet scripture teaches us there is only one God. This causes division in the church. How can scripture say there is only one God?

The scripture, which is God's word to His church, does not leave His children confused. God's word says He loves us so much that He gave His only begotten Son as a sacrifice for our sins. Then God the Son said He would go to the Father, and the Holy Spirit would come.

So in God's word, He helps us understand this better. God made humans three in one—the body, soul, and spirit. For example, as in the marriage between a man and a woman, they are joined together and become one. Get that, they are two individuals but are now one. Exchanging marriage vows requires total commitment and unconditional love. It expresses complete faithfulness to each other. That is why God the Father hates divorce; a husband and a wife are forever one until death. Matthew 19:5–6, "Therefore a man shall leave his father and his mother and hold fast to his wife, and the two shall become one flesh? So, they are no longer two but one flesh. What therefore God has joined together, let not man separate." This is the most quoted verse of scripture on two becoming one; however, there are some fifty references as well.

I think it is worth noting that Father God always has order. There is a hierarchy. We see it in the universe, His immediate family, with the angels, and the human family. God the Father is the creator of heaven and earth; God has no beginning or end. Who can understand this? No one. This is why we have atheists, agnostics, and others trying to deal with the existence of God.

An interesting note to insert here is that God instilled in the angels and human family a need to worship. Maybe that is the reason why the human family struggles with this issue, because there is a desire to worship; however, we want to do it our way. For example, throughout history, the human family has worshipped many other gods, humans, and material things trying to fill this hunger inside of us.

There are so many questions we have as we travel on our journey.

There is no time frame with God. God is eternal (Job 24:1). God created a universe so vast that it is estimated that we can only see 5 percent of it. So we ask the question, is there other life out there throughout the universe? There could be. God may have hundreds or thousands of other earths as we know it throughout His universe.

We know from the science community that the universe is so precise, and if it were not so, the earth would be destroyed.

As a child, my friend and I would lie on our backs and look into the universe and see how many outlines of stars in the sky we could see, such as the Big and Little Dipper and many more.

When we sit with a group of Christians studying scripture, we are asked to list the attributes of God. God is loving, caring, kind, and many more. I am sure John 3:16 would be noted: "For God so loved the world he gave his only begotten Son, that whosoever believes in him will be saved," but little is said. Saved from what? From hell and eternal damnation! Hell is eternal damnation—the total absence from God, total darkness, and a place of extreme suffering.

Oh, by the way, did you catch the word *study*? Yes, study. The Holy Spirit as our teacher will help us use scriptures to interpret scripture. What does that mean? Scripture must interpret itself. So when you come across scripture that may seem confusing, as you study the scripture and search for other texts referring to the same subject, you can draw a comparison and you will have a clear interpretation (Matthew 7:13, 13:37–42, 49–51; Revelations 19:19–21; and many more).

The side of Father God we must have a firm understanding of is the justice side. Do we dare to study this side of God? Yes, we must. The scripture teaches that the beginning of wisdom is fear of the Lord. Proverbs 8:13 says, "The fear of the Lord is hatred of evil. Pride and arrogance and the way of evil and perverted speech I hate." Fear not him who can destroy body, but fear him who can destroy the body and the soul (Proverbs 1:7, 9:10, 2:1-5, Matthew 10:28).

Jesus's mother, Mary, who was filled with the Holy Spirit, said, "And his mercy is for those who fear him [Jesus] from generation to generation."

Wow, we need to fear Him, and God gets really angry. Knowing who God is and His reaction to disobedience must not come as a surprise to anyone. God clearly wants us to understand who He is, and if we disobey Him, we better fear Him. This fear is a healthy fear that will help us not to miss the greatest privilege of all—*eternity with Him.* Putting fear into its proper context, the fear of God is to keep us away from something awful and harmful because those things can be eternal. For example, our parents warn us not to touch a hot stove or we could be seriously burned. They want to spare us the pain—that is love.

The angry side of God is critical to each individual but equally as important to a nation. So when we examine the decline of the United States of America, we are religious, but our gods are immorality, materialism, and other religions that are Antichrist. The results are homelessness, drug abuse, sexual perversion, open borders, and others that are eating away at the core of our nation's beliefs in the Holy Scriptures. We have lost our purpose to spread the gospel of Jesus Christ throughout the world, and Satan is at our doorsteps.

The recent call to repent has been ignored by most churches, and we will face devastating consequences. Many of our church leaders no longer believe the Holy Scriptures as the word of God and openly teach a false gospel. These leaders do not allow God's word to stand by itself and instead compromise God's word to satisfy the will of the people. 2 Timothy 4:3 says, "For the time is coming when people will not endure sound teaching, but having itching ears they will accumulate for themselves teachers to suit their own passions." This in turn leads the church community to believe that compromising and allowing same-sex marriages, homosexual lifestyles, living together outside of the marriage bond, and abortions will help stop the decline, but only the opposite will occur. This is a sad situation because the church thinks that accepting these lifestyles is showing God's love to these people. The modern-day world has changed the definition of love to mean acceptance; however, they are only condemning them to an eternal hell. People become angry and call this thinking hate speech, but it is really out of God's love for them. We must help them understand it's not what I or others think; it's what the scriptures teach (Romans 1:18–32). God says He gives them up. That doesn't mean there is no forgiveness; if one will ask for forgiveness and turn away from their wicked ways, God is just to forgive them.

We need to make sure we understand that when a nation is ordained by God to spread the gospel of Jesus Christ and we turn our backs on Him, He will seek out another nation to fulfill His commission. This is a hard truth. God will withdraw His Spirit from the nation, the people will be left in control and Satan and his demons will move in, all hell breaks loose, and the people will destroy themselves.

The people who *really love God* are those who follow the word of God in its fullness, as to what God's word is saying. If they repent and obey the teachings of the scripture, they will be forgiven and have eternal life with Him. Oh, by the way, there will be those who will become upset with what God's word has to say; that's your free will and your choice, but once you die, remember, eternity is a long time, and only God's word will stand.

So if you're a person teaching a false gospel, you may think you're making another person feel good; however, you are causing them to be eternally lost. Your punishment will be far greater when you face the final judgment.

God the Father has an intolerance for disobedience. We must understand why His Son had to pay a terrible price for our redemption. When we receive the gift of forgiveness, Jesus said, "If you love me, you will keep my commandments." This directive has far more meaning than we seem to understand. We are called to obey. God the Father's intolerance for sin does not stop when you receive Jesus as your savior; in fact, the call to obey His word becomes even more direct to the believer. When we obey or disobey His commandments, they have serious consequences one way or another. As you study the scripture and search out the word obey, you will fully understand how important and critical obedience is to Father God

We can learn from the angels. When they disobeyed, they were thrown out of His presence. Also, Adam and Eve disobeyed and were removed from the Garden of Eden as well as many others. That sounds like a simple statement, but that's a large part of God's word. He wants to help us not to make the same mistakes others have made.

These occurrences are a theme throughout scripture. Using these two accounts will open our eyes to who God the

Father is. He is loving and hateful. Hateful is pretty harsh, but God hates disobedience.

God created the human family and later sent a flood to destroy all the people, except for the few who obeyed and trusted in Him. He destroyed the people of Sodom and Gomorrah because of disobedience.

Let's get real. Is it any different today? These people were just like us, living life with their families, having parties, and living the dream. In an instant, they were destroyed by God. When we read these accounts, we do not often personalize it, but again, these were real people.

We read about Saul and David. Saul killed thousands, but David killed tens of thousands. The people they killed were real people with families. Remember when David got Uriah's wife pregnant and then tried to deceive him? When that didn't work, David had him killed. This was not just a story; this was real life.

Throughout scripture we read how God gave orders to destroy millions of people because of disobedience. We read in the later days that men and women will party and turn from God, and in an instant, He will bring judgment of destruction upon the earth. That includes us.

Our loving God says, "Enter by the narrow gate. For the gate is wide and the way is easy that leads to destruction, and those who enter by it are many. For the gate is narrow and the way is hard that leads to life, and those who find it are few" (Matthew 7:13-14). Make no mistake about it—our

God loves us, but He hates disobedience and will bring destruction upon the earth, and He means business.

Father God gives hope to the people. 2 Chronicles 7:14 says, "If my people, which are called by My name shall humble themselves, and seek My face, and turn from their wicked ways; I will hear from heaven, and will forgive their sins, and heal their land." May we hear his words for the sake of the gospel of Jesus Christ and the people.

# GOD THE SON

Jesus, as part of the God head, has made a way for the human family to reconcile man to God the Father. Without Jesus, His obedience to the cross, and His resurrection, it would be impossible for redemption. What made Jesus so special is He was not only very God but very God-man. This allowed Jesus to show total obedience to His Father but experience man's everyday challenges as an example to mankind. Jesus always shows so much compassion and love. Jesus knows our struggles and our continuous battle to obey. He knows our need for the power of the Holy Spirit to be an overcomer.

Jesus said He came to do the will of His Father. When He taught us to pray, He said, "Our Father who art in heaven." I make note of that because Jesus said pray to the Father in His name. So why do some people pray to Jesus? That's not to say we're not to talk with Jesus; it's what He taught, but we should pray to the Father in His name. This is important because Jesus loved His Father, and in love and obedience, he always put Him first, and that is what He taught us.

In Luke 2:46–47, Jesus, at the age of twelve, was sitting in the temple listening to religious leaders and asking them questions. They were amazed at His understanding of scriptures and His answers. Jesus increased in wisdom, in stature, and in favor with God and man.

In Luke 4:14, Jesus began His ministry. What He did first was go to the synagogue, roll out the scroll, and go to the scripture to reveal His coming and His purpose. Luke 4:18–19 says, "The Spirit of the Lord was upon me, because he has anointed me to proclaim the good news to the poor, He has sent me to proclaim liberty to the captive and recovering of sight to the blind, to set at liberty those who are oppressed, to proclaim the year of the Lord's favor."

As we understand this declaration, we learn as Jesus began to teach scripture and give discernment of the scripture, it brought conflict with Sadducees, Pharisees, and Scribes.

Throughout Jesus's ministry, He would rebut the Sadducees, Pharisees, and Scribes with these words: "Have you not read?" or "It is written." Jesus, being very God and very man, was able to quote scriptures and bring spiritual meaning as well. Remember, the Spirit of the Lord was upon Him.

So why is this so critical? The Sadducees, Pharisees, and Scribes were teaching the people man's rules and regulations instead of the heart of scriptures. They were religious but not filled with the Holy Spirit. If you are not of the Spirit, you cannot understand the things of the Spirit. In fact, these are the people who put Jesus to death.

Don't be surprised; if persecution comes, it will be the religious people we will have to be concerned about. God's ways are clearly spelled out, but there are religious people who are going to do it their way. Today we hear the scriptures are out of date, and if we don't keep up with the times, they will no longer attend church, so compromise is destroying the church. The gospel of Jesus Christ remains firm now and forevermore.

# GOD THE SPIRIT

After Jesus was baptized, He was led by the Spirit to be tested. Catch that, the Holy Spirit led Jesus to be tested. Through fasting and in His (the Holy Spirit) power along with scripture, Satan was defeated. The Holy Spirit will also test us.

Jesus, meeting with His disciples after His resurrection, said, "I must return to my Father but there come one after me, the Holy Spirit to be our comforter and lead us into truth." Let us make sure we understand this; the Holy Spirit will lead us into truth. If we are studying the scriptures and we hear the messages from others, the Holy Spirit will bear witness to its truth (John 3:7–8, 14:16–17).

The precious Holy Spirit is a gentleman and will not impose Himself on us. Remember free will? We have a choice to surrender to the Holy Spirit and receive God's plan of salvation or reject it. Jesus is knocking at our heart's door, and if we receive Him into our lives, the Holy Spirit will be there for us. We will not be alone, ever.

Before the Holy Spirit came, we saw how the human family failed, and now we have the Holy Spirit and the power of God in us. Some argue we are not perfect and we still disobey, in which scripture teaches that if we say we are without sin, we are liars. We all will disobey at some point, but scripture teaches that there is *willful* disobedience—that is different. What is important is if we slip up and confess our sins, we will be forgiven.

I like the scriptures teaching that says, "Thy word I will hide in my heart that I will not sin against thee." Yes, this can only be accomplished with the power of the Holy Spirit. Jesus always gives us an example of this when He was tempted by Satan. He was filled with the Holy Spirit and scripture as He rebuked Satan.

There are so many different lifestyles that violate scripture, and many people are willing to accept these lifestyles. Like there is no way out. Wrong! There will be no excuse! God gives us victory; all disobedience can be overcome through the power of prayer and the Holy Spirit and the word. Thy word I will hide in my heart, so I will not disobey you. Each believer must invite and surrender to the Holy Spirit to experience God's freedom.

To clarify this point, one must study and not just read scripture. Why is that so important? By just reading, we fall into misinterpretations. We all have opinions, but when it comes to facing eternity, others' opinions do not count. Surrender to the Holy Spirit and study His word; His Spirit will bear witness to our spirit what is truth, which will be confirmed in scripture.

Now it is clear—we have God the Father, God the Son, and God the Holy Spirit to lead us to eternal life.

1 John 2:25–27 states, "And this is the promise that he made to us—eternal life. I write these things to you about those who are trying to deceive you. But the anointing that you received from him abides in you, and you have no need that anyone should teach you. But as his anointing teaches you about everything, and is true, and is no lie—just as it has taught you, abide in him."

# ANGELS

The creation of angels are God's first creation that could communicate with Him. What we know is God gave the angels free will. Free will from what? In order to have free will, there had to be choices, so I think about what choices the angels may have and what may have gone wrong. We don't know all the choices that were given to angels, but we do know with limited knowledge from scripture that there was a hierarchy with leadership positions. One of the angels, Lucifer, was apparently jealous of Jesus and His position. Because he had free will, Lucifer disobeyed and rebelled against God along with many other angels. This rebellion eventually resulted in him and his followers having to leave heaven. Scripture teaches that one-third of the angels followed him. One-third is a significant number; we're talking about millions of angels, which will be important later on with how they affected the human family (Revelation 5:11).

This is where I violate my own rule that everything must come from scripture. Where is heaven compared with the universe? We know that earth is a small part of the universe. We also know that Lucifer and his followers are inhabiting a part of the earth. There is no information of their boundaries relating to the universe, but scripture teaches they roam the earth. The translator of scripture changed the name Lucifer to Satan and the angels that followed him to demons. So going forward we will use these descriptions and how they relate to the human family.

Satan and his demons like to live within something. Before the creation of man, there is evidence of dinosaurs and reference of Nephilims. Everything beyond that would be speculation and distracting from the purpose of the book. We also know they like to inhabit humans and animals. Luke 8:30, 13:10–16 is a must-study for a born-again Christian. Knowing who our enemies are and their impact on the human family is important. When the human family is disobedient, we open ourselves to demon possession.

Satan's desperate attempts to avoid judgment by killing Jesus failed. What's so amazing is Satan lived in the presence of God, His Creator, and wasn't able to understand who he was dealing with; our all-powerful God would eventually get sick of his behavior and disobedience, which would eventually land him and his followers into a lake of fire.

Back to the purpose of the book. Angels, both good and bad, will have a profound impact on the human family.

# THE HUMAN FAMILY

The Holy Scripture (Jesus is the embodiment of the word) is the instruction manual for the human family on how to go to heaven. This manual is very detailed on how we can reconcile ourselves to the Father. What makes this manual different is the numerous warnings along the way that will keep the reader from making mistakes. But remember, if one makes a mistake, scripture will teach you how you can get back on track. There are stories that help us learn from the mistakes of others, which are very helpful. Oh, by the way, there are also warnings that hopefully will keep us from making a fatal mistake. We need to make sure we read these warnings with extra care. God is the writer, and He gives us these warnings to help us reach Him.

So here is the deal. If you choose only part of these detailed instructions, it will lead to human interpretations and division. These instructions come with firm warnings, neither add nor subtract to the authors' instructions. When we are talking about where we are going to spend eternity, I don't want or need someone else's opinion.

Going back to the fall of Satan, we understand he had free will and was disobedient. Adam and Eve also had free will and were also disobedient. Free will gives us a choice, to obey or disobey, and it is how we relate to a relationship with God.

It is important for the followers of Jesus to understand God's expectations of how we are to live and the importance of surrendering to the Holy Spirit as our teacher and guide. Scripture teaches us if you're not of the Spirit, you cannot understand the things of the Spirit. 1 Corinthians 2:15–16, we keep this scripture in mind when we talk with those who are outside the faith. Scripture teaches we plant the seed (Jesus), we water the seed (present His word and how we live), and God does the rest. This is a process, so when we read the instruction manual, our love for others is critical for them to see Jesus.

One of the most beautiful illustrations of Jesus's love was some years ago when Mother Teresa was interviewed by a news reporter, and after answering many questions, she asked the reporter if he would like to see Jesus. With a stunned look, he acknowledged, and she took him out to the streets and found a man lying on the ground in a very filthy condition and dying. She lifted him up, put his head on her lap, and began to wipe his face and give him love. She looked up at the reporter and asked, "Do you see Jesus?"

It is very comforting that when we witness to others, we don't have to give our opinions on lifestyles or other forms of disobedience, but we must help those who are witnesses to use scripture to answer their questions.

OK, back to my point. If we were to try and defend ourselves before God, we do not want to hear these words: "It is written, depart from me!" because we lack the knowledge that comes from the word of God. Going back to John 3:16 is comforting; however, when we continue to study scripture, it becomes clear that being born again means we are new creatures, and there must be a change on how we live our lives. There is a cause and effect to be a follower of Jesus.

Just a reminder, we have free will to make choices, and those choices are clearly laid out in scripture. Romans 12:1–2 says, "I appeal to you therefore, brother, by the mercies of God, to present your bodies, as a living sacrifice, holy and acceptable to God, which is your spiritual worship. Do not be conformed to this world, but be transformed by the renewal of your mind, that by testing you may discern what is the will of God, what is good and acceptable and perfect."

# IN THE BEGINNING

## Disobedience

The human family began with free will, to obey or disobey. God created the heavens and the earth and found it good. On the eastern part of the earth, He created a garden called Eden. This was the space where God placed Adam and Eve. Outside of the garden is where Satan and his demons roamed.

In Genesis 2:9, we find a critical acknowledgment of God establishing free will and a choice between obedience and disobedience. God planted the tree of the knowledge of good and evil in a beautiful garden and gave Adam and Eve instructions to leave the tree alone, or else they will die.

God allowed Satan to enter the garden to tempt Adam and Eve. We don't know how long this temptation went on, but eventually, Eve gave in and ate from the evil tree. Then she encouraged Adam to disobey God, and then they received the consequences of their actions. The couple had to leave the garden. Not only did they now have to deal with Satan, but they also had to deal with all of the demons.

We must not move on too quickly here. Dealing with an angry God, they had to hear the consequences—the curse on the snake, woman, and man (Genesis 3:14–19). These curses are in effect today and will be so as long as the human family exists on earth.

The tragedy is their disobedience flowed over to their children and all generations to come.

For the most part, I think what happened to Eve and then Adam are again too quickly overlooked. For the believer in Jesus, there is a story here. Remember that scripture translates scripture! Satan tempted Eve, so when we forward our study, we see Jesus being tempted by Satan as well. Now let us apply this to ourselves; we, too, are and will be tempted by Satan and his demons.

A very important part of this story is that Eve gave in to Satan and disobeyed God. She did something else—she tempted Adam, who also disobeyed.

What Eve did is worth noting. Do you experience people who are drunkards or do illegal drugs try to get you to do it as well? This isn't new news. Disobedience likes company, and when we disobey and cause others to disobey, scripture teaches it would be better to put a millstone around our neck and be thrown into the middle of the sea. Why? Because encouraging others to disobey has eternal consequences. For example, scripture teaches a drunkard will not inherit the kingdom of God. So I drink alcohol with my children or friends, and one of them becomes an alcoholic and dies and goes to hell; responsibility will lie at my doorstep. I have heard the argument, "I'm not responsible for what others do." Oh yes, we are, like it or not.

Romans 14 gives us personal freedoms. As we read on throughout the chapter, God qualifies our freedom instructing us to be considerate of others by not causing them to stumble. If we do, we are no longer walking in love.

It is important not to gloss over what's happening here. We say there were consequences, but how often do we hear messages on what they are, and when do we read the entire testament of God? There is no letup. Again, those curses to the snake, woman, and man as found in Genesis 3 are still in effect today.

In a way these curses to the human family have become our tree of disobedience. Satan and his demons are suggesting to women that their husbands don't have the right to rule over them; they are equal. This position taken is disobedient. So it is with men. When men advocate their responsibilities to women, they are disobedient, and it directly has a negative effect on the family and society. Social science studies prove how both the man and the woman play such an important role in life and the lives of our children.

So as Satan tempted Eve to cause Adam to disobey, today Satan is tempting women to destroy the important role men play in family life and so on. Some may feel offended; however, women play the most important role in the life of families. They are skills managers, and their love for their family and children is much harder for men. For those who are single, Proverbs 31 defines the attributes of women that are valuable to any company. Jesus demonstrated how we should treat women. In fact, scripture teaches if we mistreat a woman, we will not get answers to our prayers.

We all have heard the term *man-made disaster* or *an act of God*. Really, we know God created the garden, which was a perfect environment. It was man's disobedience that messed things up. So the natural tendency of man is to blame someone else for their problems. When we blame God, we fail to see the real problem we're experiencing. For example, yes, God caused the flood but only because of man's disobedience to Him. God did send storms throughout history as a result of disobedience, but to describe it as an act of God relinquishes the responsibility of man.

In the life of Job, we read God *allowed* Satan to harm him and his family as a way of showing Job's obedience even in difficult times. When bad things happen, it always relates to Satan, and that is a sermon by itself. So to stay with it, is it possible to know we have eternal life? We will continue in that thought.

God came to Cain and warned him to get control of his thinking, but Cain disobeyed and killed Abel. The results of his disobedience and the consequences are still in effect today. This example is important to take note of. Cain's disobedience had long-term consequences. When we sin, our disobedience can have long-term consequences to ourselves and our families as well. If we ask, we will receive God's forgiveness, but the consequences can last a lifetime.

I would suggest that when we as a nation support the killing of our children (abortion) and sexual perversion, among other kinds of disobedience, God will discipline us not only as individuals but also as a nation. So when we experience these horrible disasters, could God be trying to get our attention? He will discipline a nation, and if we continue to disobey Him, things will get worse. In 1 Corinthians 5:5, He took the life of a person who continued to be disobedient. Oh, let's not overlook the flood and Sodom and Gomorrah. There is hope, however, found in the book of Jonah. The people of Nineveh repented, and God forgave them. 2 Chronicles 7:14 states, "If my people who are called by my name will humble themselves, and pray and seek my face and turn from their wicked ways, *then* I will hear from heaven and will forgive their sin and heal their land."

Consequences are a part of each decision, good or bad, as seen throughout scripture. We hear very little about consequences, and it's the consequences that can cause us to miss God's blessings for the individuals as well as the family. Disobedience and consequences are what I'm hoping to convey because eternity is a long time. 1 Samuel 15:22–23 says to obey is better than to sacrifice.

Now that we have that understanding, we go to the testaments of Matthew, Mark, Luke, and John. The stories of Christmas and the birth of Jesus are great, and without exception we know His birth brought us redemption. However, there are some lessons worth noting. Jesus was always obedient to His Father, even up to His death on the cross. Jesus as a very young man was about doing His Father's business. He would meet with religious leaders and was always firm when teaching the scriptures.

## Saved from Temptation

We know from scripture that God is love, but God can get really angry. We saw Jesus very God when He became angry with people selling things at the place of worship. He became not only verbal but also very physical, throwing their tables and yelling at them because this was a place of worship. I would suggest as God's children we take notice of His behavior toward disobedience. He will get angry, and He does.

OK, that's the heavy side of Jesus, then there's the side of love and compassion like that shown to the thief on the cross and the parables of those who came into the kingdom in the eleventh hour. Those stories are great, but for those who did come in at the end of their journey, they missed the joy of walking with Jesus and experiencing the power of the Holy Spirit in sharing their faith with others.

With the following background, do the scriptures give a clear understanding of how to obtain eternal life? Again, scripture teaches it is written that we may know we have eternal life. Keep reading.

So let's get started with John 3:16: "For God so loved the world that he gave his only begotten Son that who so ever believes in him has eternal life." Awesome! OK, is that all there is to it? Let's see what scripture says.

Let's take a look at man's history and give just a few examples to get a feel of man's struggles and how Jesus gave us hope. We start with Jesus. Matthew 3:16–17 teaches that Jesus was baptized, and the Holy Spirit descended upon Him. This account is absolutely a must to understand, the power given to Jesus. Remember, Jesus was very God and very man, so scripture and the Holy Spirit's power were necessary to defend Himself from Satan. Jesus's life teaches us, God's children, to use scripture and be filled with the Holy Spirit to resist Satan and his demons. When we face temptations, we can use scripture to face these moments with "It is written." I add here, if you're dealing with a particular sin, find it in the scriptures and read it every day as much as necessary, and you will find victory.

After Jesus was baptized and the Spirit came upon Him, He faced temptation, and His ministry was off and running. Jesus is our role model and our example. To summarize, He acknowledged to John the Baptist that He wanted to be baptized—this is free will. He received the Holy Spirit's power to face Satan. This is so important to the human family. Let's jump ahead to the testament of Acts, which is so important. After Jesus was crucified and rose again from the dead, He revealed Himself to His disciples and others. He gave them instructions that the Holy Spirit would come upon them, and they, too, would receive power.

OK, this is where we who believe in Jesus must really take notice. We have free will, we will be tempted, and we will be tested. Jesus faced Satan with scripture and with the power of the Holy Spirit; so must we. We, more than likely, will never deal directly with Satan. We are harassed by his demons. Why do I say that? Because Satan is not omnipresent like God is, so he is dealing directly with the more prominent people, heads of states, and those who have very successful Christian ministries. There is also a hierarchy in Satan's kingdom, and the demons who are higher up the ladder will deal with those who are making the most influence on others such as pastors, those who share the gospel with others, and so on. The rest of the demons deal with the average folks. This is why we must pray for God's protection over our leaders.

After Jesus went through the test of being tempted, He gathered His disciples, and He taught them and took them out to give them hands-on experiences. He taught His disciples by the way He lived and spoke and by showing His total obedience to His Father. Then Jesus commissioned them to go out and preach the gospel on their own.

OK, let's pause here. We see Jesus obey by getting baptized and receiving the Holy Spirit, surrendering to the Holy Spirit and the power of scripture. During this time He was constantly challenged by the religious leaders who plotted to kill Him. He was also teaching His disciples scriptures and how to live so that after His death and resurrection, they could carry on His ministry (Matthew 28:16–20). Jesus instructed His followers to go and make disciples of all nations, also reminding them that He had to leave so that the Holy Spirit would come and be our comforter and lead us into truth. This is an example for us. We need to surrender to the Holy Spirit and study scriptures so that we can be His disciples. The Holy Spirit is the only way we are able to live an obedient life.

As a born-again believer, we need to obey and be a disciple. We are now God's ambassadors and no longer live for ourselves. We live for Him, and as His disciples, we live to share the gospel with others, either verbally or through how we live our lives. God's word tells us to love others, even those whom we may perceive to be unlovely. When we show love to others, it is God's way to work in the hearts of the unsaved.

We read about John the Baptist as a forerunner to Jesus's coming and His message of repentance, which is so good, but we miss Matthew 3:10: "Even now the axe is laid to the root of the tree. *Every* tree therefore that does not bear fruit is cut down and thrown into the lake of fire." We must bear fruit and seek God to use us to fulfill His commission.

# FREEWILL

Question: Are we born with a sinful nature, or are we really born with a free will? Some say we are taught we have a sinful nature, but are we? Or is this a lame excuse to be disobedient? Adam and Eve were not created sinful; they were created with a free will to obey or disobey. God allowed Satan to tempt them, and again, with free will, they made the wrong choices, so I believe that applies to us. This begins when we are old enough to understand God's word. Earlier I made reference to the scriptures written at a third-grade level, so that can be a measuring stick. However, this varies with each child, and God will be the Judge of that. So here we may ask, what about those who have never heard the scriptures? This is one of the many mysteries of God. There is no answer, only speculation. We know from scripture that God has so many ways to communicate with the human family. He spoke through the burning bush, through animals, and even wrote the Ten Commandments on a stone. In the book of Numbers, he spoke directly to Moses and Aaron. What we have is the scriptures and that will be our focus.

When children begin their journey with free will, they will need to learn behaviors and how to make choices. So when children say no, one would say see that they're of sinful nature. No, they are learning to make choices. Scripture teaches to bring up a child in the Lord, but all children go through a critical learning experience to when they are tempted by demons to disobey God's word. At this point we should be teaching children about Bible stories that relate to free will and how they can choose to obey the scripture.

I would suggest that most parents are more concerned that their children learn the ABCs and arithmetic. We want them to become successful in their life endeavors as well as extracurricular activities. As important as this is, the primary focus must be learning God's word and their free will to make choices, to be obedient or disobedient. One is temporary and the other is eternal.

So we receive the gospel message, then what? Do we go on as before we were saved, or is there a change in our lives? Indeed, there must be a change. In Romans 8 the apostle Paul makes it clear that to continue in disobedience, God forbid. We must not continue to live in *willful* disobedience.

In the power of the Holy Spirit, we study scripture that will change our lives. Again, transforming our life from one of disobedience to a life of obedience requires the infilling of the Holy Spirit, scripture, and work. The Holy Spirit will not force His will on us. Our free will is a choice to surrender to the Holy Spirit in seeking strength to live an obedient life.

Scripture teaches that when one needs to be saved, today is the day. This is an urgent call from God because we know not when God will terminate our life or when He will rapture the church out. We don't want to be like the five virgins who weren't ready for His coming or again, in Matthew 7:12–14, be rejected from the kingdom of God.

I don't want to give any misconceptions regarding Jesus—he is the only way to God our Father and heaven. Jesus is the narrow way; any other way will lead to eternal damnation. There are so many verses that establish that as fact, but then why do so many have concerns? For some reason humans have the tendency to go overboard on how we interpret things, so I guess this is why so many fear any thoughts of working may be considered legalism and may think any works at all will disqualify them from heaven.

Old-school legalism changed our actions but not our nature. When our nature changes, so do our actions. This is why grace is so important. It's not by works less any man will boast, I get that. But scripture also says by their fruit we shall know them or work out our salvation. Below is from a devotional; in Galatians 5:19–21, Paul deScribes the works of the flesh, and they all have one thing in common—they reject restraint and resolutely abandon self-control. It is self-control that empowers us to deny the allure of the world, defy the desires of the flesh, and resist the temptation of the devil. But it doesn't stop there. As this ripening fruit nourishes in our soul, it emboldens us to walk in the Spirit and thus oppose the work of the flesh. *Let's be clear. This is not us resisting the acts of the flesh; it is God, the Holy Spirit in us exercising His self-control and His lordship over our lives!*

# OBEDIENCE

God wants His people to obey. They are redeemed, so let them live redeemed lives. They are his workmanship; let them look like it. They are new creatures; let them act as such. Self-control is a Christian essential—a distinctive! Without it the appetites of the flesh break through and besiege our lives just as Proverbs 25:28 deScribes: "Like a city whose walls are broken through is a person who lacks self-control." We are literally children of God instead of children of men. As we walk in the Spirit, we can live on the level of the supernatural instead of the natural, following spiritual rather than fleshly desires, for we live in the Spirit instead of the flesh. Paul admonished us to "walk by the Spirit, and you will not gratify the desires of the flesh" (Galatians 5:16). As we do, the Spirit's self-control will grow fragrant and strong in our lives, restraining the flesh with its destructive passions and releasing the power and life of God that we might "work while it is still day."

Let's see if this can be better understood. Person number one is consciously trying to please God by doing things. There is never any peace because there is fear they're not doing enough. Person number two is working for the kingdom because of what Jesus has done for them and the love they have for Him by taking up their cross in obedience to fulfill his word. Get the picture? One does because they feel they have to; the other does because of respect and love for God.

We read in scripture the account of Cain and Abel. God was pleased with Abel's sacrifice but not with Cain's. To get a little more graphic, if we had any part in our salvation, we would all go around heaven telling how we made it or bragging. That would not be good. We will reach heaven through our love for God and through Jesus for His obedience to His Father and for paying our debts. Oh, don't let me forget our precious Holy Spirit—our teacher and our guide. It's all three that will bring love unspeakable and full of glory. So we, along with the angels, will gather around the throne and sing, "Holy, Holy to the Lord God Almighty."

I sidetracked, so back to my concerns. Just believing in Jesus, is that enough? For each of us, only God can judge the heart of a person. Only a person can know if they're born again by the Spirit and the study of scriptures. Emotions, as great as they can be, go up and down. Only the scriptures and those who are obedient can give us assurance (John 3:1–21).

# LIVING FOR CHRIST

John 3:36 says, "He who believes in the Son has eternal life, but he who does not *obey* the Son shall not see life, but the wrath of God abides on him."

Did that say he who does not obey the son shall not see life? That is where studying comes in. We read John 3:16 as a predicate, but then there is more. If you love me, you will keep my commandments; by their fruits you shall know them. If you do this or that, you shall not inherit the kingdom of God. In the last days, there will be a falling away from their faith, or when persecution comes and that cloud is now on the horizon, will we be able to endure? If you deny me, then I will deny you. Wait a minute. I asked Jesus into my heart; He cannot deny me. Brothers and sisters all over the globe, Christians, are denied food and a place to live as well as being martyred in the name of Jesus. Are you spiritually ready for that? That takes preparation, putting on the whole armor of God to fight the good fight, and if that hour should come and in the power of the Holy Spirit, we are told not to say a word but only as the Spirit gives utterances (Mark 13:11). Five of ten virgins were prepared; are you?

There are many teachings in scripture that must cause us concern, such as Matthew 7:1–29 and, in particular, verses 21–23. Could we consider that these people believe in Jesus?

As a refresher, let's consider Matthew 25:1–13. Could we consider these people as believers in Jesus? Again, Jesus teaches us about the ten virgins. Question: Did they believe in Jesus? Of the virgins who were waiting for His coming, five were ready, five were not. Those who were ready entered into the kingdom of God, while the door was shut for those who were not ready. Are we getting ready? How?

The following are the major concerns:

Hebrews 10:31. It's a terrifying thing to fall into the hands of the living God.

1 Timothy 4:1–4. In later times some will depart from the faith.

2 Timothy 3:1–9 gives a list of those who will not inherit the kingdom of God—lover of self, lover of money, proud, arrogant, abusive, disobedient to parents, ungrateful, unholy, heartless, unappeasable, slanderous, without self-control, brutal, not loving God, treacherous, reckless, swollen with conceit, lover of pleasures rather than lovers of God, having the appearance of godliness but denying the power. Then there are the parables of the sowers of the seeds and the weeds (Matthew 13:1–42). Matthew 15:10–20 defines what is in the heart. In these verses, Jesus says, "Hear and understand: it is not what goes into the mouth that defiles a person but what come out of the mouth; this defiles a

person." Jesus defines other behavior issues as found in 1 Timothy 6:3–10, Ephesians 5:1–21, and so many more.

Let's take Malachi 3:1–18. We like to read how loving God is; however, when it comes to giving our tithes and offerings and we decide not to give, we seem to think we get a bye. Pastors who know they need money to advance the gospel of Jesus teach in an apologetic way. They must quit apologizing; this is a command from God.

Let's examine Malachi 3, not in part but as a whole. Verse 8, will man rob from God? Yet you are robbing from me. But you say, "How have we robbed from you?" In your tithe and offering. Verse 9, get this, "You are cursed with a curse for you are robbing from me, the whole of you." We don't read verses 8 and 9. Why? We like verses 10–12, where we are blessed. Back to the seriousness of verses 8 and 9 and read Acts 5. Ananias and Sapphira who kept back some of their proceeds and were struck dead. Many people suffer death and illness from robbing from God. We have a choice to obey or disobey.

Suppose you left your money on the table to be used to pay for essentials and your child took it and spent it foolishly. Then it happens again and again. Would you say to the child, "Please stop stealing our essential money?" So to help stop the child from stealing, you tell them they can take small steps so that hopefully they will stop. I don't think so. You would sit down and tell them to stop it, and if it didn't stop, there would be discipline. Believe me, it wouldn't take long before it would stop. So God says if you rob from Him and if you don't stop, there will be a curse upon you. People misunderstand when God blesses them financially. They see bigger houses and more material things. *No!* They are blessed to give more to the kingdom, to bring more into His kingdom. There are many scriptures that teach that the love of money will lead us to an eternal hell. In Luke 12:16-21, we read about the rich man and all his barns, and then what?

Deuteronomy 8:11-20 illustrates the danger of God blessing His people and His people misusing His blessings. When God blesses us, He is trusting us to use our blessings to further the Gospel.

So this is redundant, but is there any hope? In 1 John 5:13, God says, "These things I have written unto you that believe in the name of the Son of God; that we may know we have eternal life."

So once we receive salvation, the next important step must be taken. 2 Timothy 2:15 says, "Study to show thyself approved unto God a workman not to be ashamed dividing the word of truth a right."

When Jesus rose from the grave, He put Satan under His feet. Satan knows the clock is ticking and his time is short. He and his demons have been judged and will be sent into an eternal lake of fire. Satan and his demons are seeking whom they can devour and take with them. So now more than ever, born-again believers must get into the scripture's teachings to stay obedient. He that endured to the end will be saved. To endure is a fight and requires scripture and the power of the Holy Spirit. Again, this is free will, so make the right choice. Choose ye this day whom you will serve; you cannot serve two masters.

Jesus, before He ascended into heaven, assured His followers that He had to return to His Father, and the Holy Spirit would come to teach, comfort, and give power to His followers. So without the infilling of the Holy Spirit, the disciples fled in fear, and once they saw Jesus had risen from the dead, Jesus instructed them to pray and wait to receive the Holy Spirit. When the Holy Spirit came upon them, they were filled and spoke with other tongues as the Spirit gave them utterances. These were believers from different countries speaking in their own language. When the Holy Spirit came upon them, they spoke in tongues allowing them to all understand each other.

Catch this: after the Holy Spirit came upon them. Acts 4:18–20 says they couldn't stop speaking what they saw and heard. In the power of the Holy Spirit, the disciples went out speaking boldly, and as we read in scripture, they died for the sake of the gospel.

OK, we received Jesus as our Savior, and we are filled with the Holy Spirit. God's word now is our direction of God's expectations as to live an obedient life. I can't emphasize this enough. We hear preaching, which is good, but by studying the scriptures with the Holy Spirit as our teacher, we will be able to discern truth, which is so important. Remember to hear these words: thou good and faithful servant, a life of obedience is absolutely essential.

So as a review, God gave the angels free will to obey or disobey, as He did with the human family. God gives the human family help, so if we choose, we can surrender to the Holy Spirit, and He will give us power to an obedient life. God's gift of the Holy Spirit leaves us without excuse to *willfully* disobey His word. The scripture gives a specific list of what pleases God and what makes Him angry, so there will be no excuses. Study to find yourself approved.

OK, I know that no one is perfect, so if we travel on our journey and slip up, God is forgiving, but make sure you understand *willful* disobedience. What scripture says about *willful* is so important.

So now for those who fear legalism. Jesus said, "If you love me, you will keep my commandments." (John 14:15). The words *love me* must permeate our being. To love God with all our hearts, soul, and might is a firm understanding of the price God paid for our redemption, and to please Him should be no questions. To obey His commands is not legalism but a manifestation of one's love and respect for God. God loves obedience rather than sacrifice.

When we give our hearts to Jesus, we no longer live for ourselves. We are His ambassadors; we now represent Him. How we live and what we say will affect others. Scriptures teach if we love the things of the world, we are enemies of God. Why is that? When we love anything such as our families or the world, it is all for self-satisfaction, which is temporary. Loving God is eternal.

If you need understanding from a pastor or a teacher on the scriptures and they say, "Let's see what the scriptures say," you're with the right person. However, if they say, "This is what I think," and it doesn't support scripture, beware and run away. 1 John 4:1–6 says to test the Spirit to see if they are from God.

I would add here, to those who are responsible to preach and for all of us who are responsible to share the gospel, we must never mislead another person.

Remember on Judgment Day, what is in scripture will be the only thing that matters.

How important is this? Again, Romans 14:20–23 and Luke 17:1–4 warn if we cause a person to stumble, it would be better to put a millstone around our neck and be thrown into the middle of the sea.

It is written you may know you have eternal life. Do you have a passion for others and those who are lost? We should have a desire to reach others for Jesus by the way we live our lives and share with others as well as give our offerings to the church so that as the body of Jesus Christ, we can reach others both at home and throughout the world. That will in turn reflect on our love for Him.

We have millions of demons running around and about us, busy tempting us to destroy our witness for Jesus. In 1 Peter 5:8, in fact, there are hundreds of scriptures about Satan and his demons roaming the earth, seeking whom they can destroy. So can we say the devil made me do it?

Absolutely not. Satan and his demons can tempt us; however, we have free will to obey or disobey, so that takes away our excuses.

Through the power of the Holy Spirit and scripture, the apostle Paul in Galatians 5:1–25 and Philippians 4:8 give only a few of the many verses instructing God's children how to walk in the Spirit. If we live by the Spirit, we are not under the law but living by faith.

Prayer is an important part of a believer's life. Pray without ceasing. We can talk with Him anytime and all the time, and as we draw closer to Him, God continues to speak new revelation through His word. The Bible is the only book you can read over and over and constantly increase in knowledge.

Jesus taught us how to pray, and it's called the Lord's Prayer. I'm not sure how the title the "Lord's Prayer" was given, so I would like to suggest because Jesus taught us to pray it would give more meaning if it was referred to as the "People's Prayer." Jesus gave it to the church, which is an all-encompassing prayer. There's an important distinction here. Jesus, as very God-man, understood and was able to experience what we face in our everyday life, so He taught us how to pray for a reason.

We are to pray as an acknowledgment to our Father who is in heaven and give praise to His holy name. It is His kingdom we are looking forward to and His will to obey. He supplies all our needs according to His riches in heaven and expects us to help others. We are expected to forgive others as we have been forgiven. We end with a recognition of where we get provisions and our power. It is the perfect prayer. Jesus gave it to us so that we would realize there is great significance to it.

Life is dynamic with so much of it we don't have any control. What happens in individual lives can and will be tested and disciplined by Father God.

# HEAVEN

Oh, how we like to sing about heaven. Heaven is a wonderful place filled with glory and grace. Indeed, it is. Scripture gives us many glimpses of its splendor. I like that song, filled with glory and grace, because we will experience God's love, which one cannot even describe. Just think about it. We will be in the presence of our Father, Savior, and Comforter throughout eternity.

Let's see. Who is going to get there? Are you? It is written you may know, and it is God's way. God wants all His creations to be eternally with Him—that's the purpose behind John 3:16. The question we must all ask is, do we want to be there? Are we living like we want to be there?

Like I have stated, God created the angels and the human family with free will. So in heaven there will also be free will. God's word is filled with instructions on how to spend eternity with Him. Like so many men, we start putting things together, and then when it doesn't work, we read the directions. If we don't understand even after we read the directions, there is a hotline to call the manufacturer to get help. After all, we spent a lot of money, didn't we?

OK, so we want to go to heaven, and we open up the scriptures (directions) on how to get there. Sometimes we may not understand what God means.

Father God took care of that problem. Romans 10:13–17 states the importance of having a pastor who is filled with the Holy Spirit and uses the scriptures to help in your understanding. The most expensive gift we will ever own is God's Son.

The joy of heaven will be when all of God's children are gathered at the throne of God singing praises to Him. Everyone is totally committed to Him.

When you go to a worship service and everyone is singing their heart out in worship and praising God, it's so awesome!

Have you ever gone to a sporting event and everyone is wearing their team's clothing and sitting on the same side cheering your team on? That may seem a little weak to illustrate a religious example, but if you have ever been in a stadium with one hundred thousand fans cheering, you know what I'm talking about. There will be joy unspeakable and full of glory.

OK, I got carried away for a moment, so let's get back to God's word. God says, "You cannot serve two masters," so what does that have to do with heaven? (Matthew 6:24) Don't read over that too quickly. That's profound in so many words. In fact, next to the gospel, it has significant importance. You are choosing the one you wish to live for. God is demanding complete commitment to those who will be with Him in heaven.

The scriptures are full of references that clearly teach. Once you choose your master, there are serious consequences either way. That doesn't mean if you choose Father God as your master, there won't be difficult times, as we read in Romans 7.

Let's turn to Revelation and study the seven churches. Father God says, "I know your works." What He says is really hard to read, especially when He says to the church of Laodicea, "I know your works: you are neither cold nor hot. Would that you were either cold or hot! So, because you are lukewarm, and neither hot nor cold I will spit you out of my mouth" (Revelation 3:15-16).

So why would He say that? In heaven only the hot (totally committed) will spend eternity with Him. The choice of making Father God your master and your passion to serve Him here on earth will continue throughout eternity. Your passion of thankfulness for His only begotten Son and the precious Holy Spirit will fulfill our presence with Him. That will bring a presence of joy unspeakable and full of glory. Our thankfulness will allow our free will to be steadfast throughout eternity.

I would like to leave it there, but at the end of the word to the Laodicea church, Jesus says, "He who has an ear, let him hear what the Spirit says to the church. Are you listening?"

As scripture interprets scripture, John 3:16 says that whosoever believes in Him has a cause-and-effect component, which is so important. Allow your faith to trust and obey, for there is no other way to be happy in Jesus.

Matthew 7:24 says everyone then who hears these words of mine and (does them) will be like the wise man who built his house on a rock.

# WORSHIP

**To the born-again believer,** what does Father God's words say regarding the Sabbath, also known as the Lords Day?

Genesis 2:1-3, "The Seventh Day God Rests; Thus the heavens and the earth were finished, all the host of them. And on the seventh day God finished his work that he had done, and he rested on the seventh day from all his work that he had done. So, God blessed the seventh day and made it HOLY, because on it God rested from all his work that he had done in creation."

Exodus 20:8-10, "Remember the Sabbath day, to keep it HOLY. Six days you shall labor do all your work, but the seventh day is to the Lord your God. On it you shall not do any work, you, or your son, or your daughter, your male servant, or your female servant, or your livestock, or the sojourner who is within your gates."

In the beginning, we are given clear instructions regarding the Sabbath.

To continue the theme that scripture interprets scripture, in Numbers 15:32-36, "while the people of Israel were in the wilderness, they found a man gathering sticks on the Sabbath day. And those who found him gathering sticks brought him to Moses and Aaron and to all the congregation. They put him in custody, because it had not been made clear what should be done to him. And the Lord said to Moses, "The man shall be put to death; all the congregation shall stone him with stones outside the camp." And all the congregation brought him outside the camp and stoned him to death with stones, as the Lord commanded Moses."

Going along further in the scriptures we see Jesus dealing with the Pharisees, Sadducees, and Scribes. These church leaders took the word "work" to mean everything, including doing good, on the Lord's Day. So, Jesus attempted to get them to understand the difference from work and doing what was necessary on the Lord's Day. He says that a day of worship, eating, and other necessary activities that require attention are ok.

In Mark 2:24-28, Jesus teaches of the Sabbath and states, "The Sabbath was made for man, not man for the Sabbath. So the Son of Man is lord even of the Sabbath" (Mark 2:27-28).

Early on, churches met daily and thousands of people were added to the church. Then, the human family, once again, started to interject their rules and requirements. The formal church evolved from meeting daily, to when I was a young child in the 1940's meeting twice on Sunday's as well as participating in Sunday school. On Wednesday nights we had prayer meetings, and on Saturday's we went to Catholicism class in the morning and Youth for Christ at night.

The progression continues today, in most churches we're down to one service on the Lord's Day. Instead of a day of worship and rest, we keep our businesses open causing us to turn away from God and focus more on materialism and personal pleasure. The human family will soon realize the consequences for their disobedience to God's requirements to rest on the Lord's Day.

Throughout all of scripture we are given a firm understanding of God's revelation to worship. So as born-again Christians, can we neglect our desire to worship? Our hearts must hunger and thirst for righteousness. If we lack that desire, we must step back and examine our relationship to our Heavenly Father.

A simple analogy for this is when a baby is born, they cry for milk and eventually solid food. As it should be with a born-again Christian. When we recognize our sinfulness and repent and receive Jesus into our hearts, our thankfulness and love for Him will cause us to hunger for a closer relationship to Him. At first, we drink the milk of the word and then the meat, by living a life reflecting the love of God and becoming His disciples sharing the gospel with others.

I read a recent article which made reference to two great teachers of the scriptures and their definitions of worship. MacArther's simple definition (The Ultimate Priority [Moody Press 147]): "Worship is all that we are, reacting rightly to the way He is."

While William Taylor gives a more thorough and eloquent definition: "To worship is to quicken the conscious by the holiness of God, to feed the mind with the truth of God, to purge the imagination by the beauty of God, to open the heart to the love of God and to devote the will to the purpose of God." (ibid. p147)

Worship is when we realize how great God is and how small we are. So, we should meet regularly with the Saint's on the Sabbath to worship Him.

Sin slowly brings the human family into disobedience regarding the Lord's Day. Disobedience has and will bring serious consequences to ourselves, families, and our country. We must repent of this sin and return to worshipping our great God and Savior.

# FINAL NOTE

As a child, I would listen to the adults arguing about their views of what they believe regarding the scriptures. Sometimes it could get rather uncomfortable and appeared to strain their relationships. Why the arguing? Scripture interprets scripture. It's the "I believe" that gets in our way.

Why is this so disturbing? In the beginning of Jesus's ministry, we read how He sat in the presence of religious leaders, teaching from the scriptures what was pleasing and displeasing to God. The leaders constantly challenged Jesus's teachings, but Jesus would call them out as hypocrites. These religious leaders brought divisions among the people, leading many to eternal damnation. Their hearts were filled with self-righteousness, and they were blind to the truth.

They divided themselves into different sects—the Sadducees, Pharisees, and Scribes. Today we do the same, only worse. In the faith community, we have hundreds that fit into those three categories, with most blind to the simple truths of the gospel of Jesus Christ and its great commission (Matthew 28:16–20, Mark 16:15–18, Luke 24:44–49, and John 20:19–23).

Some say they are Baptist, Protestant, Catholic, Methodist, Quaker, Church of God, Pentecostal, and most recently, Independent and many more. When you read a list of all the different denominations, you realize Satan has infiltrated the churches and has taken our eye off the great commission to bring the gospel of Jesus Christ to the lost.

Think about it. We have the teaching of Jesus right in front of us, and as religious as we are today, we still stumble in darkness. Why? First Corinthians 2:14 says, "But the natural man receives not the things of the Spirit of God: for they are foolishness unto him: neither can he know them, because they are spiritually discerned." The spirit of disobedience says, "I'm doing it my way."

Let's see what Jesus has to say about the behavior of the Sadducees, Pharisees, and Scribes. Read the following scriptures: Matthew 23:13, 23, 25, 27, 29. But woe to you hypocrites! Verse 16, Woe to you, blind guides.

What Jesus said didn't change the religious leaders; in fact, they were the ones who had Him crucified.

Jesus is saying to these people, "You have lost your purpose. You are self-righteous and love yourself." This is offensive to Father God.

Here are a few examples. My wife and I sat with a couple in our place of worship, and when communion was served, they refused and said they would only take communion from their church. Really? What would a church building have to do with communion? You don't have to be in a specific building to remember what Jesus did for us. In fact, you can take communion at home if you understand biblical instructions before you take part in it.

In my high school social studies class, there were ministers from different denominations that would come to address our class. We had a Catholic priest address the class, and he was asked how the Catholic Church felt about interfaith marriage. He was strongly against it. His reasoning being that either person who will agree to accept the other's faith, they are putting themselves and their religion before God. Different gods. What was he talking about?

These are just a couple of examples, and there are many more, that illustrate how far we wander away from Jesus's teachings. We should be one body working together to share the gospel of Jesus Christ. That will save the lost.

Study the ministry of Jesus and how He taught His disciples; love your God with all your heart and soul and your neighbor as yourself. You cannot possibly expand on that. He challenges us to avoid foolish arguments and ideas, reminding us we are all neighbors and that we all need Jesus Christ as our savior. OK, so what did Jesus say to these leaders? Reading Matthew 23, He pronounces seven "woes" on religious leaders, so what would He say to us?

To differentiate the life of Jesus from the Sadducees, Pharisees, and Scribes, Jesus loved all people no matter what their circumstances. He was deeply criticized by who he would hang around with. The Pharisees and Scribes would isolate themselves thinking they were better than others.

Jesus saw through their hypocrisy and pointed it out to them. Can we parallel that today within the religious community?

We have so many different denominations, but what about our educational institutions? We have public schools, Christian schools, and private schools.

I think this would be a good place to inject Matthew 5:13–16. Jesus said, "You are the salt of the earth. But if the salt loses its saltiness, how can it be made salty again? It is no longer good for anything except to be thrown out and trampled underfoot."

You are the light of the world. A town built on a hill cannot be hidden. Neither do people light a lamp and put it under a bowl. Instead, they put it on its stand, and it gives light to everyone in the house. In the same way, let your light shine before others that they may see your good deeds and glorify your Father in heaven.

As a youngster attending a public school, we had to say every day out loud the Ten Commandments and the Pledge of Allegiance to the flag of the United State of America.

Congress took God out of our school systems, and it was with little resistance. Would that have happened if the church community was fully involved? Again, was the salt removed from the school systems?

As a body of Christ, we function better when we're together. As a born-again believer, the only title we must have is we are God's children. We must have one purpose, which is to love God with all our hearts and our neighbors as ourselves and share the gospel of Jesus Christ to the world.

The old cliché says there will be no Baptist, Protestant, or Catholic in heaven, only believers in Jesus Christ. That is absolutely true. Are we so foolish to think we are going to go to heaven based on our denomination? Satan has attempted to divide God's children with different denominations, and he did it. In fact, we're still doing it today. New churches are popping up everywhere. If it is done to draw closer to communion, that is fine, but if we are divided by anything other than sharing the gospel of Jesus Christ, we are Sadducees, Pharisees, and Scribes. We must be able to sit with our brothers and sisters in Christ and remember what the Lord Jesus Christ did for us on earth and in heaven.

Jesus tried to teach the religious leaders the truth and was killed for it. We should be focused on being the salt of the earth and sharing the Gospel of Jesus Christ to the lost and dying world.

When Jesus taught His disciples the message of the gospel, it was simple but so profound; it is eternal. Love God with all your heart, keep His commandments, and share the gospel with others.

Study the teachings of Jesus found in the gospels and Galatians 5, 1 and 2 Peter, and 1 and 2 John for a precise and clear understanding of God's requirements to know who are His children and how we are to live. Note the word obedience as you study, as it's so important.

A personal story: as a child, a few friends would get together and get into mischief. One of our friends, Steve, would always go home before we would get into trouble.

Some years later I asked Steve what caused him to go home when we started getting into trouble, and what he said was so profound: "I went home because I had too much respect and love for my parents." Could we parallel that with our relationship with God? Why do we obey God? Because we respect and love Him with all our hearts. If God's children had that kind of relationship, it would absolutely change us individually, as it would the church.

What Jesus taught was simple but hard. The great commission found in Matthew 28:16-20, "Now the eleven disciples went to Galilee, to the mountain to which Jesus had directed them. And when they saw Him, they worshiped Him and some doubted. And Jesus came and said to them, 'All authority in heaven and on earth has been given unto me. Go therefore and make disciples of all the nations, baptizing them in the name of the Father, in the name of the Son, and in the name of the Holy Spirit, teaching them to observe all that I have commanded you. And behold, I am with you always, to the end of the age.'"

Believe in the Lord Jesus Christ and thou shall be saved. Jesus said, if you love me, you will keep my commandments. His commandments are deep and reach into the heart. Jesus said, the commandments say thou shall not commit adultery, but I say if you look upon a woman and lust in your heart you have committed adultery. The commandments say; Thou shall not commit murder, but I say if you hate your brother you have committed murder in your heart. These are hard truths, but scripture teaches, thy word I will hide in my heart so I will not sin against thee. It is our heart that defiles a person. How is your heart?

As we share Jesus, find comfort, my brother and sister. In 1 Corinthians 3:6–8, Paul writes, "I planted the seed, Apollos watered it, but God has been making it grow. So, neither the one who plants nor the one who waters are anything, but only God, who makes things grow. The one who plants and the one who waters have one purpose, and they will each be rewarded according to their own labor." As God's children, we are working with Him, and He will bring the increase.

# IN CHRIST LOVE!

I hope this book stimulated thoughts as to where we will spend eternity and gave you a greater desire to draw closer to God. Oh, by the way, then He will draw closer to you (James 4:8). Remember the ten virgins—five were prepared and five were not. Now is the time to prepare. When being filled with the Holy Spirit and your knowledge of scriptures, it will keep us ready for His coming and/or in death. We can be ready as the five virgins were.

Repent of your disobedience and receive the Lord Jesus Christ as your Savior. Surrender to the Holy Spirit, pray without ceasing, and study scripture to find yourself approved. Share the gospel of Jesus Christ with others. The certainty of life is we will all face death, but the question is, where will we spend eternity? You have free will to choose, and again, we will only have one opportunity to get this right, so obey scripture, love God with all your heart, and love your neighbor as yourself. Think about it. Scripture teaches that an eye has not seen or ear has not heard what He has for those who love Him. Then we with two-thirds of the obedient angels will stand before the throne of God and sing, "Holy, Holy, Holy to the Lord God Almighty." That's going to be awesome!

> Little children, let no one deceive you. Whoever practices righteousness is
> righteous, as he is righteous. Whoever makes a practice of sinning is of the
> devil, for the devil has been sinning from the beginning. The reason, the Son
> of God appeared was to destroy the work of the devil. No one born of God
> makes a practice of sinning, for God's seed abides in him; and he cannot keep
> on sinning, because he has been born of God. By this it is evident who are the
> children of God, and who are the children of the devil: whoever does not practice
> righteousness is not of God, nor is the one who does not love his brother (1 John 3:7–10).

# IT IS WRITTEN

Have you ever missed out of events because you heard of it too late and all the tickets were sold out?

The ticket to heaven will only sell out once we die, so get yours before it's too late. Information on how to get your ticket is found in this book: *Jesus Said, "I Never Knew You."*

With all the new technologies and activities available to us, we have lost the art of spending quiet time reading and studying the scriptures. These active lifestyles put us in danger of being so involved in the temporary that we may miss the eternal.

There is a serious generational decline in church attendance, which eventually leads to a moral breakdown and historically has proven the destruction of many great societies. There are studies that show there are progressive steps that society will go through before the end comes. Proverbs 1 and Romans 1 also give us insight of the progressive results of disobedience to God.

*Jesus Said, "I Never Knew You"* invites you to embrace the word of God, the Holy Bible. It will fulfill the precious words "If you draw close to me, I will draw close to you" (James 4:8 and Jeremiah 29:12–14).

The author, Larry K. Vliem, graduated from Aquinas College. He served as an elder and deacon of his local church as well as taught Sunday school. He is a retired management staff from BASF Corporation, where he worked for thirty years. He is married and has three children.